A MESSAGE FROM SCHOLASTIC INDIA

Hello there, my friend!

Like the rest of the world, I'm sure you've been stuck at home. Online classes just aren't the same as school, are they? How have you been spending your time at home? Have you tried cooking and baking? I know I have!

Let me assure you, once you've read this book, Pinkoo Shergill is bound to inspire you to experiment in your kitchen. So get your spatulas, pots, pans and imagination ready to impress your family with some delicious desserts and a little mayhem!

Shantanu Duttagupta
Publisher

PROLOGUE

Some people are born with silver spoons in their mouths. Pinkoo Shergill, however, was born with a spatula, a palette knife, a whisk and a cake smoother in his hands. Most people have a sweet tooth. Pinkoo Shergill, on the other hand, had all sweet teeth (and, ahem, a couple of cavities too). He lived, breathed, loved, slept and dreamed desserts. Quite naturally, whipping up a three-tier cake was, well, a piece of cake for him.

There he was now, spreading a large dollop of white chocolate buttercream on the top of a cake. His tongue was sticking out of his mouth—it always did when he was concentrating hard on something. And he was expertly going about his business.

Lightly brushing the surface of the cake with strawberry syrup. DRIP! DRIBBLE! DRIZZLE!

Rotating the cake on the turntable and applying the buttercream icing on the side with a palette knife. SPREAD! SMEAR! SMOOTHEN!

PINKOO SHERGILL PASTRY CHEF

'Fun, uplifting, laugh-out-loud read that questions and challenges a range of stereotypes in an easy-going manner'

— Myth Aunty, library educator

'*Pinkoo Shergill Pastry Chef sparkles* with energy and life'

—Varsha Seshan, author

'Vibha's crackling dialogue and Shamika's rib-tickling illustrations make this story ... a delight'

—Lavanya Karthik, author and illustrator

'A fun, fun, fun book that upends a lot of stereotypes with a delightfully light touch'

—Jaya Bhattacharjee Rose, Ace Literary Consulting

'With its upbeat prose, this one is sure to inspire young ones to experiment in the kitchen'

—*eShe* magazine

'A thoughtful and funny book'

—*Teacher Plus* magazine

for ABCDT

Published by Scholastic India Pvt. Ltd.
A subsidiary of Scholastic Inc., New York, 10012 (USA).
Publishers since 1920, with international operations in Canada, Australia, New Zealand, the United Kingdom, India, and Hong Kong.

For information regarding permission, write to:
Scholastic India Pvt. Ltd.
A-27, Ground Floor, Sigma Centre
Infocity-1, Sector 34, Gurgaon-122001 (India)

First edition: June 2021
This reprint edition: November 2023

ISBN-13: 978-93-90590-87-2

Printed in India at Sai Printo Pack Pvt. Ltd.

PINKOO SHERGILL

Pastry Chef

written by

vibha batra

illustrated and designed by

shamika chaves

SCHOLASTIC

New York Toronto London Auckland

Sydney New Delhi Hong Kong

Pushing a couple of wooden sticks into the cake till they touched the cake board. PLUNGE! HOLD! SUPPORT!

Placing wax paper on the bottom tier, carefully stacking the middle tier, and then, the top tier.

Adding luscious decorations—edible flowers, rainbow sprinkles—around the bottom and along the sides. PRETTY! YUMMY! COLOURFUL!

Covering the top of the cake, every inch, with plump gleaming strawberries. FRESH! RIPE! JUICY!

He managed to add the finishing touches to his DROOLASTIC masterpiece in the nick of time.

BUUUZZZZZ! Rang the buzzer.

The judges hurried over to judge.

Oh, the breathless, suspenseful wait!

'... And it's a perfect ten!' The commentator roared as the judges held up the score paddles. 'Oh my goodness! Pinkoo Shergill has done it! He has made Olympic history. He has bagged the gold in the Bake-a-Thon event. This is the first time India has won a medal in this fiercely contested category.'

The stadium erupted into a TREMENDOROUS applause.

'YOWZAAAA!' Pinkoo plucked off his pristine white baker's hat and tossed it into the air. It somersaulted like a graceful gymnast, before landing back on his head in a perfect finish.

He joined his hands, bowed low and came up blowing sloppy, smacky, squishy kisses at his adoring fans. A roar went up as he whipped his T-shirt over his head and flung it into the crowd. The spectators went totally, completely, fully berserk. 'Pinkoo! Pinkoo! Pinkoo!' They chanted at full volume.

He closed his eyes, savouring his victory. It felt warm, rich, delicious. Kind of like a freshly baked apple pie.

'PINKOO! O PINKOO! PINKOOOOOOO puttar!'

Pinkoo's ears pricked. Wait a minute, that didn't sound like his fans.

In fact, it sounded like someone closer home.

It sounded like ... oh no, it was Mummyji.

GROAN!

CHAPTER 1

Pfftt went Pinkoo's dream.

Mummyji was chanting his name, engaged in what appeared to be a wrestling match with the blankets (and at this point, the blankets seemed to be winning).

'The boy has swaddled himself like an Egyptian mummy,' she muttered, yanking

off a blanket only to reveal another thicker blanket.

And who could blame Pinkoo. It was like the ice age in there. There were two fans and one AC in the room, all running on full blast. (There were three reasons why he wanted his own room. This was Reason Number Two. He wanted to sleep like a normal human and not hibernate like a woolly mammoth.)

'Come on, Sleepy Singh ... you don't want to be late again ... there's no time, no time at all ...' As Chachiji's squeaky panicky voice drifted into Pinkoo's ears, he burrowed deeper into the covers.

Meanwhile, Mummyji gave a hard tug, finally pulling the last blanket off him. 'You have to be at the shooting academy in fifteen minutes.'

ARGHHHH! Shooting had shot down his favouritest dream. Once again.

'But I don't want to be at the shooting academy,' Pinkoo protested, wresting back control of the blanket and pulling it over his head. Not in fifteen minutes, not ever, he added to himself.

'Okay, fine, be like that ...' Mummyji trailed off, a warning note in her voice. 'I know what to do.'

'I say we hit him with my Nerf gun,' suggested a little girl, her voice as steady as her aim.

Pinkoo shivered under the blankets. It was Tikki, his cousin sister. She was almost six and already the most violent person in the entire history of the universe.

'I've a better idea,' Mummyji said, dropping her voice to a low whisper.

'Cold bottle of water coming right up, Tayiji,' piped up Tutu, Tikki's brother.

Under the covers, Pinkoo gritted his teeth. Tutu was one year his junior and one big pain in the neck. And he was also his roommate and Reason Number One. (Reason Number Three? He was almost ten. Surely, he needed—deserved—some privacy.)

Obeying Tayiji's command like a well-trained Pomeranian, Tutu bounded out of the room.

Pinkoo waited. For Tutu to come galloping back, for the sheet to be rudely whipped away, for Mummyji to flip him onto his back, for an icy cold splash to hit his face. He steeled himself for the Arctic attack. It never did come, but Papaji's steely voice sure did. 'Pinkoo?'

That was all the motivation Pinkoo needed. PINNGGGGG! He cast the covers aside, leapt from the bed and dived straight into the washroom. All in one swift, seamless motion.

'Like a bullet whizzing towards to its mark,' Mummyji remarked, torn between admiration and exasperation.

Tutu shook his head. 'Same story. Every. Single. Day.'

'Oh, shut up, Tutu,' Pinkoo snapped from the other side of the door.

'I was supposed to be visiting Mamaji, spending my holidays in Canada,' he grumbled grouchily, as he emerged half-awake but fully dressed. 'But here I am, waking up in the middle of the night, being dragged to that awful place, day after day. This is the WORST SUMMER EVER!'

That made Mummyji go 'awww'. 'It's not so bad, is it?' she asked gently.

'It's worse. To the power of infinity.'

'It's only for one more week,' she consoled Pinkoo. 'Then school will reopen ...'

'... and we will have to wake up early for school,' he finished grimly.

'What's taking you so long?' came Papaji's papad-crisp voice. 'Are you coming?'

Sir, yes, sir! Pinkoo nearly clicked his heels before taking to his heels.

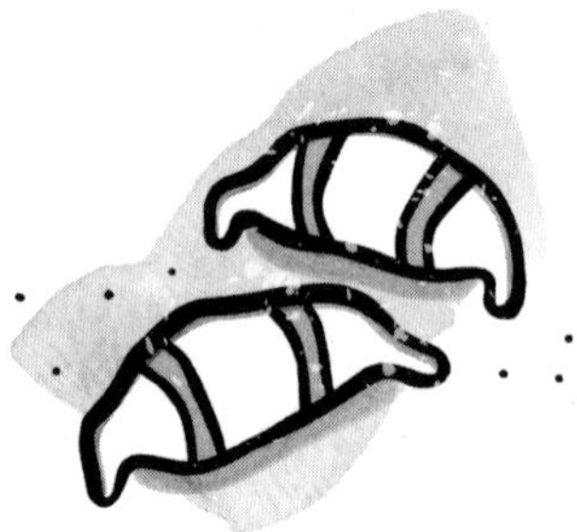

CHAPTER 2

'Let's go,' Papaji said to their long-time chauffeur, Raghav bhaiya, as he slid into the passenger seat. According to highly placed sources (okay, according to Raghav bhaiya himself), his grandfather used to drive for the Maharaja of Patiala.

Squashed in the back seat of their SUV, between Chachaji and Tutu, Pinkoo felt a royal headache coming on.

'So, how are the shooting classes coming along?' Papaji asked no one in particular.

Pinkoo opened his mouth to mutter a suitably safe reply. He had some options on the tip of his tongue:

1. Oh, they couldn't be better.
2. FABTASTIC!
   WOWMAZING!
   SPECTACULOUS!
   We're ready for the Tokyo Olympics.
3. Gold medal, here we come.

Unfortunately, Tutu beat him to it, throwing safety to the wind. 'Coach says we could do a whole lot better, Tayaji.'

SMACK! Pinkoo nearly slapped a hand to his forehead. He swung his head sharply to the right and glared at his cousin. Tutu gulped.

If eyes could speak, here's how the conversation went:

PINKOO'S EYES: 'You did not say that out loud!'

TUTU'S EYES: 'S-s-sorry. It slipped out.'

PINKOO'S EYES: 'Just zip up, will you? Not another word. Got it?'

TUTU'S EYES: 'Yup.'

PINKOO'S EYES: 'Ha! That was a test! You said another word.'

Tutu's eyes: 'But—'

Pinkoo's eyes: 'There, that's another word ...'

And on and on the eyes would have gone if Papaji's voice hadn't interrupted them. 'What do you mean?' he demanded, glancing over his shoulder to get a better look at a rapidly reddening Tutu.

The poor boy! He squirmed like a wriggly worm in his seat. His uncle's eyes were boring holes into him, holes bigger than any bullet could ever make.

As Tutu struggled to come up with an answer, a geography lesson came flashing into Pinkoo's mind. Natural disasters and man-made disasters. You couldn't really do much about natural disasters. But you sure could prevent GIGANTEROUS man-made ones. Pinkoo knew what he had to do. He had to think on his feet. He had to control the damage created by the boy-made disaster. And he had to prevent it from reaching epic proportions.

Too late! He lost way too much time thinking. Tutu, on the other hand, lost no time blabbing. 'Coach says we are not doing our best ... we need to concentrate ... like, really, really, really focus.' Like a mugpot vomiting all the answers during an exam, he blurted everything out.

'If only Coach stuck pastries and red velvet cakes and Swiss rolls on the target boards.' Tutu sighed. 'Pinkoo paaji would hit the bullseye each time ...'

WHOOOOSH!

A HORRENDEROUSLY horrified Pinkoo nearly rocketed through the sunroof like an ISRO satellite.

Papaji blinked in confusion. 'What's that now?'

'... Because he's a Master Ch—'

'Master Shooter!' Pinkoo bellowed, drowning Tutu out.

His roar startled Raghav bhaiya and the SUV went flying over a speed bump. THUMPPPP!

'And he loves ba-eeeeeee!' Tutu cried out in pain as Pinkoo pinched his thigh.

'Eating,' Pinkoo gasped, 'because I love eating.'

'What's going on back there?' Papaji demanded, craning his neck.

'Nothing!' The Shergill siblings said with one voice.

'For a moment I thought Tutu said baking,' said Papaji, mercifully training his eyes back on the road. 'A boy baking!' He snorted. 'What a perfectly preposterous idea!'

'Yeah, totally prepost ... err,' Tutu agreed nervously, glancing from his uncle to his big brother. 'I mean, that's not why Pinkoo paaji hangs out in the kitchen all the time—'

JAB! Pinkoo's elbow shot out to poke Tutu into silence.

'That's because I'm hungry all the time,' Pinkoo said, his voice shrilly, shrieky, shaky. His heart was thumping like a djembe.

Luckily for him, Papaji seemed to buy the story. 'Right. Because the kitchen is no place for a boy.'

The rest of the journey passed in catch-drop (think IPL match, last over-last ball) silence. Presently, Raghav bhaiya braked to a halt outside Shergill Cycle Store.

'I agree with Coach Ahluwalia,' said Papaji, turning around (fully, this once) and pinning Pinkoo with a full-on frosty look. 'It's time to think less about pastries, more about pistols. Less about red velvet cakes, more about rifles—'

'Less about Swiss rolls, more about shooting,' Tutu chimed in dutifully.

'So, are we going to follow in Grandpa's footsteps and become shooting champs?'

Pinkoo nodded, looking as miserable as he felt.

'Are we going to win the World Shooting Championship? The Olympic gold? The Arjuna Award?'

'Yes, Papaji,' Pinkoo replied, looking as if he had been awarded a prison sentence.

'Drop them at the range,' Papaji instructed Raghav bhaiya as if it wasn't their daily routine. As if they hadn't been doing exactly that for the last few weeks. Every day. All summer.

With a loud moan, Pinkoo slumped against his seat.

CHAPTER 3

Papaji got down at the store, and lo! Raghav bhaiya underwent an instant personality change. He went from bullock cart driver to Grand Prix racer. In one second flat. **ZIP! ZAP! ZOOM!** Off he sped like Lightning McQueen.

Pinkoo wanted to tell him, 'No rush', 'Take your time', but the traffic light did the job for him. They turned red without warning and

DHADANGG!

Bhaiya did manage to brake, but the bike behind them didn't.

One dented bumper (which the boys promised to keep from Papaji), one loud yelling match (bhaiya and biker, tied) and one nanosecond (at least, that's how fast it felt) later, the boys were at Hot Shotz, Patiala's oldest and most reputed shooting range. Owned by none other than—drum roll, please!—one-time Olympic hopeful, national shooting champ, serial winner of medals, shields, trophies and every sporting award out there—the one and only Naman Grewal.

Minutes later, the boys really did look like hotshots—in protective glasses and ear muffs and what not. Soon, they found themselves face to face, erm, face to potbelly with Coach Ahluwalia, better known as Coach Aloo. (Oh, not because he loved to gobble potatoes. But because his tummy wobbled like a sack of potatoes.) 'Ready?' he asked in a grumpy, grouchy, growly voice.

'Not really,' Pinkoo muttered under his breath, taking aim.

THAYN! The pellet shot out of the ten-metre air pistol, narrowly missing the target.

Not bad, Pinkoo congratulated himself, feeling quite pleased.

Coach, of course, looked anything but. 'Oh Pinkoo, we were this close,' he lamented, touching his index finger to his thumb. 'No. No. No. You're not here.'

'He's right here, Coach,' Tutu replied, waving a hand in front of Pinkoo, just like a magician does (you know, when he's about to make a person disappear).

'I mean, where's your mind?'

On YouTube. On the COOLSOME baking tutorial I saw last night, cake-mad Pinkoo almost replied. But wisely, he held his tongue. Papaji was friends with Coach, after all.

'You are physically present, mentally absent, boy—'

RUMBLE! His empty stomach registered its presence, too.

'Let me guess,' Coach Aloo broke off to shake his head. 'Let me guess, you skipped breakfast.'

'He woke up late. Again. Jumped straight from the bed to the loo to the car. Again. There was hardly any time to—' Tutu broke off mid-sentence, looking at the forbidding expression on his Big Bro's face.

'Pinkoo, how many times have I told you,' Coach switched to Lecture Mode, 'it's impossible to concentrate on an empty stomach. Your mind needs food to function.

Would your car run on an empty fuel tank?'

'Maybe, you know, if we pushed it hard,' Tutu ventured tentatively.

Coach heaved a heartfelt sigh. 'You can do it, Pinkoo, if you put your mind to it. But it's like you don't even want to try. It's like your heart's not in it at all.'

Bullseye! Pinkoo said inside his head.

'It's been over a month and you're making the same mistakes. Over and over again,' Coach droned on.

'I'm so sorry. It won't happen again,' Pinkoo said in his most earnest voice. At least not until tomorrow, he added to himself, fighting off a cheeky grin.

'You have so much potential. You can be right there.' Coach pointed a finger skywards.

'Up in the trees?' a voice sneered behind them. 'Like a monkey?'

Pinkoo rolled his eyes. He didn't need to turn around to know who it was. Every superhero needs a supervillain to beat to a pulp. That's where Daljit came in. He was Eric Killmonger to his Black Panther. Colonel Zod to his Kal-El. Bane to his Batman. (The beating to a pulp bit, however, was yet to be accomplished.)

Daljit was also two years his senior in school and a fellow triggerman.

BUZZ! Coach Aloo's chest started vibrating. No, no, not because Daljit emitted gamma rays or something.

With a supervillain, that's always a possibility. But, in this case, there was a cell phone in Coach's chest pocket.

He stepped away to take the call and Daljit stepped up on his game (of being super villainous, what else). 'You shoot like a girl, Pinkoo,' he smirked NASTICIOUSLY.

CHAPTER 4

'Of course not,' Pinkoo retorted. 'All the girls in our age group are crack shots. Me, I'm not even close.'

It was true. Pinkoo wondered why people said such stupid stuff like that. Guess Mummyji was right. They WERE dumb. They didn't know any better and they didn't want to learn.

'Top. Top. I mean, Pinkoo can be right at the top,' Coach explained, returning to the scene.

Doctor Octopus snorted.

'And he will be,' Tutu crowed, like any loyal sidekick would.

Just not at shooting, Pinkoo added silently. He mentally tuned out of the sport and logged into baking. What was he going to whip up for dessert today? Crumbly, crusty, melt-in-the-mouth chocolate cookies? Light, fluffy, velvety lemon tarts? Sugary, sticky, oh-so-soft jam rolls?

His spirits soared at the thought. He couldn't wait to rush back home, throw on his apron and try out a new recipe. Oooh!

A thrill ran down his spine, his hands positively trembled and he started glowing like a Glo Worm.

'See, that's what I'm talking about.' Coach watched Pinkoo's face flush with excitement and jumped to the wrong conclusion. 'If thinking about winning feels so good, imagine how good winning will feel.'

'Sweet,' Pinkoo replied without thinking.

'Sweet? BLECHH!' Daljit sniggered in his ear. 'You're such a girl, Pinky.'

Coach turned to him. 'Okay, sonny boy, let's see what you have got.'

'Watch and learn, losers,' the Meanie Marksman hissed.

BANG! The pellet found its mark as if there was a magnet stuck to the target board.

'Told you,' Daljit gloated. 'I'm a crack shot.'

'Crack pot,' Pinkoo muttered.

'I mean, there's "jit"—victory—in my name.' The evil one laughed because what's a supervillain without his trademark sinister laugh.

'There's also "dull",' Pinkoo pointed out.

'Now, now, boys,' Coach interjected, 'where's your sporting spirit?'

'My turn,' trilled eager beaver Tutu-ster. 'Prepare to be amazed.'

Thwack! The pellet was like a car without GPS. It ended up reaching nowhere near its destination.

'Wow! That *was* amazing,' Daljit said mockingly. 'You are so bad, you are good.'

For once, Pinkoo had to agree with Venom. But, like any good brother (and superhero), he kept his mouth firmly shut.

'Don't worry,' Coach said in a reassuring voice, 'we've got all morning. Your Tayaji called and asked if you both could stay back for some extra coaching.'

THUDDD! Pinkoo almost dropped the pistol on his foot.

Could the day get any worse?

*

Apparently, it could.

It was around noon when their SUV drew up outside Coffee Oye—the most

FUNERIFFIC,

WONDERLICIOUS,

YUMMYSOME

coffee shop in town. Their thick shakes were awesome. And ice creams were AWESOMER. But the desserts, mmmm, they were the AWESOMEST.

There was just one teeny weeny not-so-nice thing about it, Pinkoo thought, racing up to the glass doors.

BUMP!

He collided into someone head on, sending something flying up in the air.

AAAAAH

SWOOSH! CLATTER!
SPLATTTT!

'Aaaaaaa!' the teeny weeny not-so-nice thing yelped in dismay. The tray she was clutching—the one with half a dozen, colourful, smiley faced cupcakes—was now face down on the floor.

Pinkoo immediately put on his 'I'm So Sorry' face. Partly, because he was sorry to see cupcakes get wasted. But mostly, because he so didn't want to annoy the owner of the coffee shop.

It was sad but true. Nimrat—the Most Annoying Creature in the Animal Kingdom—owned Coffee Oye.

Unfortunately, she went to his school, too. Fortunately, she was in the next section.

Pinkoo was always quick to point out that he didn't have anything against her. It was just that she was a Miss-Know-It-All who treated everyone like they were Good-For-Nothing-At-All. Why, during the school play rehearsals last year, she'd made life **GINORMOUSLY GROSSASTIC** for him. So what if he kept mispronouncing 'caravans of camels' as 'caramels of carvans'? It was a toughie, tricky, tongue-twisty phrase.

A loud SCREECH broke into his thoughts. 'PRABHJOT SHERGILL! WHAT'S WRONG WITH YOU?'

What's wrong with you, Nimrat, he wanted to yell back. Why did she call him that? Yes, it was his name. His real name. But no one called him that. Not his family, not his friends, not his teachers (okay, they did—when they were taking attendance, but that didn't count). Even Doctor Doom Daljit called him Pinkoo, for god's sake. But for Coffee Oye's sake, he kept mum.

'Oops, sorry! I didn't see where I was going.' He bent down to help her scoop up the shapeless smashed-up stuff off the floor.

'Look what you made me do.' Nimrat glared at him, dumping the Playdoh-type mess back on the tray. 'This is all your fault.' She looked as though she wanted to beat him.

'We'll pay for it,' Pinkoo said without missing a beat. It would blow a huge hole into his savings, but some mistakes have to be paid for.

'You'd better,' she shot back, thrusting the tray at him.

CHAPTER 5

'We?' Tutu protested. 'I was nowhere near the scene.'

'I meant the royal "we",' Pinkoo snapped.

'What's the royal "we"?'

Pinkoo gnashed his teeth. *Why? Why? Why was he always stuck with Tutu?* 'Kings and Queens refer to themselves in plural.'

Tutu was terribly confused. 'But why are you doing it, paaji?'

'If the history lesson is over, the cash counter is that way,' Nimrat interrupted, narrowing her eyes.

'We know where the cash counter is,' Tutu scoffed. 'We come here every week.'

'Whatever.' With that, Nimrat whirled on her toes and stomped away into the kitchen.

'That's no way to treat your regular customers,' Tutu clucked, an injured expression on his face.

'Just be happy we get to stay customers,' Pinkoo muttered, making a beeline for the billing counter.

'She's not even the real owner,' a miffed Tutu sniffed.

ZWINGGG! The doors of the kitchen swung open and out strode the real owner of the coffee shop. Nimrat's father.

'Pinkoo! Tutu! How are you?' He flashed them a broad smile, hurrying over to the cash counter.

'All good, Rajvir Uncle,' the boys chorused.

Pinkoo deposited the tray on the counter.

Rajvir Uncle peered at the contents of the tray. 'And what do we have here?'

Ever since he was a baby, Pinkoo was called Pinkoo because he had impossibly

pink cheeks. But now, his cheeks turned even pinker. 'Erm, long story, Uncle.'

'Pinkoo-Nimrat accident. Cupcakes ruined. Paying price,' Tutu supplied the short-cut version.

'Ho! Ho! Ho!' Rajvir Uncle cracked up like an out-of-season Santa. 'No worries. It's on the house.'

Pinkoo's face lit up like an out-of-season Christmas tree. 'Thanks so much, Uncle.'

Why couldn't Nimrat be half as sweet as her father, he wondered. Why did she have to be as bitter as a neem leaf? Her name should be 'Neem-rat', he grouched inwardly.

*

It was cake o'clock! Pinkoo's favourite time of the day. Because Papaji and Chachaji were away at work. Because Beeji was at Gymkhana Club—she never missed her afternoon session of cards. Because everyone else had retired to their rooms—Mummyji to catch up on her reading. Chachiji to forward WhatsApp messages to everyone on her contact list. Tikki to do whatever it is that fearsome little bandits do in their spare time.

Which meant, he could haunt the kitchen without fear of being caught white-handed (his hands would be smeared with flour, remember?)

Leaning over the kitchen island, he whipped the batter with an electric beater.

'Why don't I do it for you,' Gurdasji, their long-time cook suggested kindly.

'Allow me,' offered Datthi bhaiya, Gurdasji's helper.

But the Super Chef wouldn't hear of it.

'May I?' Tutu offered.

'Don't even think about it.'

You see, Pinkoo was baking (rather, he was trying to bake) a caramel nougat cake for Manu, his bestest friend in the whole wide world. He was back in town after one whole month. And Pinkoo wanted to treat him to his favourite dessert, but he was starting to feel a little tired after the lengthy shooting practice.

Wait a minute. What were Coach Aloo's favourite words? Yup! 'When the going looks tough, just close your eyes and visualize victory. It will give you a high dose of energy.'

Pinkoo closed his eyes and did exactly that. Imagined surprising Manu with the Happy No Occasion cake. Imagined Manu's face lighting up like an LED bulb. Imagined Manu digging into it, a blissed-out expression on his face. Imagined everyone around giving him a standing ovation.

That's it.

He started whipping the butter and

sugar with a fresh burst of enthusiasm.

CREAM! CREAM!

CREAM!

In he tossed the eggs,

one at a time.

BEAT! BEAT! BEAT!

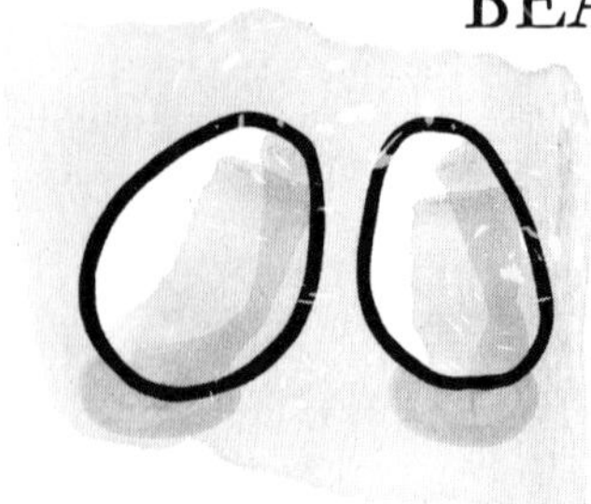

Then came the turn of the vanilla essence.

STIR! STIR! STIR!

Hot on its heels came the flour and baking soda mixture alternating with buttermilk.

MIX! MIX! MIX!

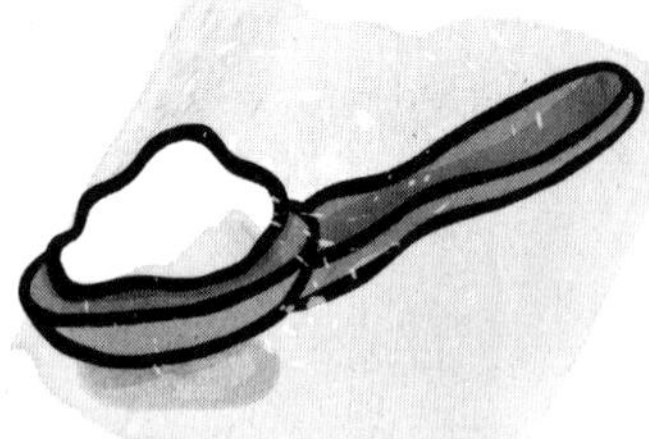

Followed by the melted caramel and nougat chocolate bars.

WHISK! WHISK! WHISK!

He paused and looked around. His forehead scrunched. 'Where's the pan? I thought I'd greased it and kept it right here ...'

'You mean, this?' Tutu asked, holding up the missing pan.

One lick, erm, look at the pan and Pinkoo blew up. 'You licked it clean!'

CHAPTER 6

Was there no end to his cousin's foolishness (and greed), Pinkoo seethed. Kitchens were high-stress environments—he'd watched enough cookery shows on TV to know that—and Tutu was not making things any easier.

'Give that back,' he growled, reaching out to snatch the pan. 'Out! Out of my kitchen. Right now!'

Tutu shuffled out with a heavy heart and heavier feet.

Pinkoo greased the pan all over again, poured the batter into it and placed it in the preheated oven.

'S-s-sorry, paaji,' Tutu said earnestly from the kitchen door. 'Please don't send me away. Trust me, I'll be the best susu chef ever.'

Pinkoo goggled at that. 'The what?'

'Susu chef. You said the junior chef was called that—'

KA-CHING!

The penny dropped. The confusion cleared. 'Oh, you mean, the sous chef. It's pronounced soo. Soo.'

'That's what I said. Susu.'

Pinkoo sighed. 'There's only one soo, Tutu.'

At this point, Gurdasji felt compelled to speak up. 'There are three susus. He, me, Datthi.'

'Oh, forget it,' Pinkoo muttered.

'Please, paaji,' Tutu pleaded. 'Promise I'll behave.'

And he did.

He didn't go YUMMM when Pinkoo brought out the cake from the oven.

Didn't go YAYYY when it passed the toothpick test—sticking a toothpick into the cake to check if it comes out dry. Dry = done.

Didn't SLURP loudly as the pastry chef stirred the glaze.

Didn't SQUEAK, not even a wee bit, when paaji drizzled the glaze all over the cake.

Didn't SMACK his lips as Big Bro sprinkled chopped walnuts on it.

Didn't even SQUEAL when the senior Shergill fixed the personalized BEST MATE topper he had specially ordered from Chandigarh.

Pinkoo looked up from his YUMMILICIOUS creation. 'Looks smashingly spectacular, doesn't it?' He grinned. 'If I do say so myself.'

As if in reply, a spot of drool escaped

Tutu's mouth and dribbled down his chin.

*

COO-COO-COO-COO-COOOO!

Standing outside Manu's house, Pinkoo rolled his eyes. Cuckoo doorbells were so IRRITATINNOYING.

'Cool,' Tutu grinned, looking impressed. 'We should get one of those.'

Before Pinkoo could open his mouth, the door swung open.

And Ninja Katori stood there. Now, Manu had not earned the nickname due to his awesome ninjaness. Nopesy-daisies. It was all thanks to his trademark katori cut. What's a katori cut, you ask? It's when you place a katori, a bowl, on someone's head and cut off their hair in the shape of the bowl. Why Manu let the barber do that to him each time was a mystery no one had ever been able to solve.

'Oyeee! What's up, yaar!' Manu exclaimed. The boys bumped elbows and wiggled their fingers at each other in the 2.0 version of the handshake.

'Hey, how was Delhi?'

Before Manu could reply, Pinkoo's Mini-Me peeped out from behind him. 'Paaji has a surprise for you.'

Manu's face split into a broad smile. 'Avengers Trump Cards?'

Pinkoo frowned. Is that how well his best mate knew him?

'Not the Quadcopter drone?' Manu asked, his excitement skyrocketing.

'Wrong!' Tutu burst like a leaky pipe. 'He baked you a cake!'

'Oh!' Manu blinked in surprise. 'But Mummy's banned all junk food. She wants me to eat healthy.' He pouted, squeezing his belly. 'All that overeating at Nani's house.'

Seeing the crestfallen look on Pinkoo's face (and remembering that Mummy wasn't home), he quickly added, 'But it's just cake. It has eggs and cream and sugar and nuts. I mean, it's practically health food.'

'Now we're talking!' Pinkoo's frown finally turned upside down and he hurried back to the car to pick up the box of 'diet' food.

*

As cakes go, it wasn't too big. Just about the right size for three (very) hungry kids.

'MMMMMM! This is to die for!' Manu said between mouthfuls. 'This can't possibly be home-made. You picked it up from Coffee Oye, didn't you?'

SWOOSH! An ecstatically elated Pinkoo nearly puffed up like a helium balloon and floated to the ceiling.

'You should be on MasterChef India, paaji.'

'That's a cookery show,' Manu corrected Tutu. 'You mean, he should be on The Great Junior Bake-a-Thon.'

'If only I could participate in it,' Pinkoo said wistfully. 'If only I could fly away to London.'

'Too bad you don't have wings.' Manu clucked in sympathy. He paused for a beat, then said ever so casually, 'Good thing, they are coming to India.'

Pinkoo was so FLABBERGASTOUNDED, he started choking on the mouthful of caramel nougat cake.

CHAPTER 7

Manu sprang to his feet and started thumping his friend's back. 'Hey! I know I said the cake was to die for. But you don't have to take it so literally!'

'Wh-wh-what did you say?' Pinkoo asked in a strangled voice, his heart beating like a nagada.

Manu's eyes danced with excitement. 'They are coming to India! Launching auditions all over the country. East, West, North, South. It was in the papers. Give me a second, will be back.' He dusted the crumbs off his shorts, sprang to his feet and dashed to the door. 'Hey, save me some,' he yelled at Tutu who was stuffing his face at the speed of light.

Pinkoo's heart! It was racing faster than a bullet train. His mouth! It was drier than the Gobi desert. His hands! They were clammier than frogs on a rainy day. Was Manu playing a prank on him? Or was the show really coming to India? Was he really this close to attaining his biggest dream? Of becoming a pastry chef? A world famous one, at that?

'Ta da!' Manu skipped back into the room, waving a newspaper clipping.

Like champion fielder Yuvraj Singh, Pinkoo made a flying leap at it. HOWZAATTT! He read it at the same speed at which Tutu was eating. Then, he slumped against the sofa, a mixture of shock and awe on his face. 'Oh. My. God.'

It was true! All of it! His biggest dream was now well within his grasp. All he had to do was reach out and grab it. Oh, there were more questions in his mind than a question paper. He tossed the one uppermost in his mind. 'What, you read the papers now?'

Manu hee hee-ed. And proceeded to narrate the entire incident. Last week, back in Delhi, he was gobbling down a crusty, flaky, spicy samosa, when BAM! His eyes fell on the newspaper that was doubling up as the plate. 'Baking Madness, Kiddos'—the headline leapt at him. He immediately leapt up and saved the 'paper

plate' (after demolishing the samosa, of course).

'Oh! That explains the grease spot.' Pinkoo hastily returned the oil-stained clipping to its owner.

Manu rolled it up and held it aloft his friend's head like a baker's hat. 'And the winner of The Great Junior Bake-a-Thon is ... Pinkoo Shergill!' he said in his best imitation of a reality show host.

Now, Pinkoo had been told that he looked kind of funny dancing (several times, by several people). 'Like a baboon doing the bhangra.' But did he care? Did that stop him? No prizes for guessing the correct answers!

'YIPEEEE!' He jiggled his butt. 'It's one whole month away. Like I need that long to prepare. Oh, I'll check out their website, but I know the format of the contest by heart.' Indeed, he knew it better than all the subjects at school. 'All I need to do is show up at the audition and—' He paused abruptly as something struck him. He sat down on the sofa heavily, looking paler than a vampire with jaundice.

Manu was concerned. 'Hey, what's wrong? Are you okay?'

'The auditions,' Pinkoo said quietly, 'they are in Chandigarh.'

'So what? It's only an hour and a half away. You can always ask Raghav bhaiya to drive you—oh!' Manu broke off mid-sentence as realization dawned. 'You'll have to break the news to your family.'

Pinkoo nodded glumly. 'To Papaji. And we all know how he'll react. He'll blow his top, go through the roof, explode like a hydrogen bomb.'

Manu felt a stab of frustration. 'I don't understand ... what's his problem with baking?'

'Not with baking. With me baking. According to him, boys don't bake, boys don't cook, boys don't do anything fun, basically.' Pinkoo sighed. 'He wants me to become like Pitaji—our grandfather. He was a national level shooter. He wanted Papaji-Chachaji to become shooters, too. Papaji had even started training ...'

A troubled look came over Pinkoo's face as he launched into the tale that had been drilled into him since he was knee high. '... He was a wiz with the ten-metre rifle, the best student at the academy. Everyone was hundred per cent sure he was going to qualify for the Olympics, become the first Indian shooter to win the gold medal ...'

Manu leaned forward, agog. 'Then what happened?'

'Pitaji fell sick ... he had cancer ... he went to God. And Papaji was forced to drop out of the Academy and join the family business straight out of school. He was the oldest son, after all. He had to take care of his family. So, it was bye-bye shooting, hello Shergill Cycle Store.'

CHAPTER 8

'And now Papaji wants you to fulfil his dream,' Manu concluded the sad saga.

'But I want to fulfil my dream,' Pinkoo said sadly. 'I want to become a pastry chef.'

'And I want to become a DJ,' Tutu chimed in.

Pinkoo rolled his eyes. Just last month, his cousin wanted to become a gamer. A lion tamer, the month before that. And god knows what before that. Hmmpf! He changed his mind faster than Chachaji changed his cell phone covers.

'I've even thought of my professional name,' Tutu rambled on. 'DJ TuTu. DJ Turban Tunder. Isn't that cool?'

'Wicked,' Manu said, with a wicked gleam in his eyes.

Pinkoo coughed. 'Coming back to the show, Papaji must never know.'

'Then you know what you have to do.'

Pinkoo's eyes widened. 'Drop out of the show?'

'No, silly.' Manu smiled. 'Keep the plan to yourself. Keep your family in the dark.'

The colour came flooding back into Pinkoo's face. 'That could work.' His mind worked furiously. 'I could always say I was going to Chandigarh with you and Uncle and Aunty—'

Tutu cleared his throat.

'And Tutu,' Pinkoo added grudgingly. 'For a day out or something.'

'Cool, we'll work something out,' Manu agreed. 'But remember, the most important thing—keep the entire operation under wraps.'

Tutu's eyes widened. 'Operation?'

'Mission, Tutu, mission,' Pinkoo

explained. 'You know what? We should give it a codename.'

'Mission Impossible?' piped up Tutu only to receive a dirty look from the older boys.

'How about PSPC?' Pinkoo thought aloud. He liked the sound of it instantly.

'Sounds like a dreadful exam. Like the UPSC or something,' Manu said with a light shudder. His parents wanted him to sit for it (when he was older, of course) and become an IFS, IAS or, at least, an IPS officer.

'PSPC. As in, PINKOO SHERGILL PASTRY CHEF.'

Manu flashed him a thumbs up sign. 'The most important thing is to treat it like the World's Biggest Secret. Think you can do that for one whole month?'

'I know I can,' Pinkoo replied. 'The multi-million-dollar question is ... can he?'

Two pairs of eyes swung accusingly to the left. Making Tutu keep his mouth shut was going to be tougher than making a hippo wear a swimsuit.

Pinkoo shot him a stern look. 'Tutu, do you want to tag along with me everywhere? Do you want to come to Chandigarh? Do you want to watch a TV show live?'

Tutu, whose mouth was full of cake, could only nod.

'Then you know what you have to do,' Pinkoo warned, zipping his lips.

Tutu pinched his throat in a solemn swear.

Pinkoo rubbed his palms excitedly, his heart racing like a Ferrari, Lamborghini, Maserati. He had a great feeling about the whole thing. Oh, he could definitely pull it off.

YOOHOO! Life was cool!

*

BOOHOO! Life was cruel!

It was the first day of school and Pinkoo had just discovered that:

1. Students of all sections had been shuffled. **Awful!**
2. He wasn't going to be in the same section as Manu. **Dreadful!**
3. He was going to be in the same section as Nimrat. **Frightful!**

Now, sitting in the last row of his class, he wondered what other horrors awaited him.

'Children, I want you to pick your own desk partner.' His class teacher, Gurdeep Miss smiled, shaking a bowl filled with chits. 'But I also want to play fair. So let's play a small game, shall we? Pick up your chit, pick up your partner.'

She walked around to the right side of the class and handed the bowl to a student.

When it was Pinkoo's turn, he closed his eyes, said a small prayer (Anyone but Nimrat, please God), and then snatched up a chit.

He sneaked a peek. And instantly saw stars.

That's because a

TREMENDEROUSLY

terrorized Pinkoo nearly shot out of the classroom window like a misguided missile.

Why did he have to sit in the last row? Why did he have to pick that chit? Why was life so unfair? For once, he was asking all the tough questions instead of his teachers. Like always, there were no easy answers.

So he did the only thing he could. Before anyone could see the chit, he quickly crumpled it into a ball and popped the paper laddu into his mouth.

'Okay, class, let's begin,' Gurdeep Miss prompted.

One by one, his classmates started calling out the names on their chits. Till only two students were left.

'I-I can't find my chit, Miss,' Pinkoo gulped.

'It's okay,' Gurdeep Miss said. 'Everyone's got their partner. There's only two of you left. Which means, you are partners. Go sit with her.'

CLANGGG! He dragged himself to the first row, feeling as though there were hundred-kilogram weights tied to his ankles.

'Didn't help, huh, swallowing the chit?' Nimrat remarked calmly, the second he flopped down next to her.

CHAPTER 9

What a DREADIBBLE first week!

First, Pinkoo had discovered that—**GASP**—the Great Junior Bake-a-Thon guys had tweaked things for the Indian edition. (How dare they? It was the format of a world famous reality show, not the school syllabus.)

Second, Pinkoo had realized that he was now hopelessly un-prepared for the auditions.

Third, Pinkoo had found out that their desk partner was supposed to be their project partner for History.

And now, instead of drowning his sorrows by baking a fresh batch of mocha almond fudge cookies, he was jetting off to the shooting academy. No, he couldn't take it anymore.

He leaned over and tapped Raghav bhaiya on the shoulder. 'Turn around, bhaiya, let's go to Manu's house.'

'But it's Friday,' the chauffeur reminded him. 'You have shooting coaching after school.'

'I'm not in the mood for shooting,' Pinkoo snapped.

'Me neither,' Tutu added, fiddling with the knob of the car stereo. The song 'Golmaal, golmaal, everything's golmaal' came on.

Raghav bhaiya glanced at him in the rear-view mirror. 'So, what do you want me to do?'

'I want you to call Coach Aloo and tell him ...' quickly thinking of an excuse, Pinkoo said, '... we have a flat tyre.'

Raghav bhaiya looked as though the air had gone out of him. 'What if Papaji finds out? No re baba no. It's too risky.'

Pinkoo took a deep breath. He knew what he had to do. He didn't want to do it.

He really wanted to avoid it. But he didn't really have a choice.

'How will Papaji find out, Raghav bhaiya? Do we ever tell him anything? Take that accident at the traffic light. Did we tell him about it? About that dent you made in the bumper?'

The chauffeur's eyes popped out like the buttons of a tight shirt.

Pinkoo went on. 'Papaji suspects Chachaji because he's such a rash driver. Imagine if he finds out the truth. But he won't. Because we won't tell him. Because we can all keep secrets. Right, Tutu?'

'Right,' Tutu mumbled, turning the knob and changing the radio station. 'Galti se mistake' blared out.

Raghav bhaiya's face went white as a blank answer sheet. 'This is not good, Pinkoo bhaiya,' he croaked.

This is blackmail, Pinkoo said silently.

*

Ten minutes later, they were sitting in

Manu's room, chomping on paneer pakodas and slurping chocolate milkshakes.

'And then Nimrat said I shouldn't tax my brain too much and leave everything to her.' Pinkoo poured his heart out to his best mate. 'I hate it. I hate being her classmate and desk partner and project partner.'

Manu was sorry to hear of his classroom troubles. 'And how are preparations for the audition going?' He asked, hoping to cheer Pinkoo up. ALAS! The query had the exact opposite effect.

'I'm not going to make it, Manu. I'm going to get disqualified in the first round.'

'What happened, Pinkoo? Calm down, tell me everything.'

So Pinkoo did. There were going to be three rounds. (These are not the official names of the rounds, just how Pinkoo thought of them, mind you.)

SHOW-OFF ROUND: All the contestants had to flaunt their baking skills. Any dessert they were SPECTACUSATIONALLY good at. Easy peasy choco greasy.

EXAM ROUND: All the contestants would be given the same instructions and the same ingredients. And asked to make the same thing. Which would then be graded on a scale of 1 to 10.

50-50 ROUND: The contestant had to come up with a dessert that was part Western, part Indian, totally YUMMIFUL. Just what did they have in mind? A Banoffee pie barfi? A phirni pannacotta? A kulfi custard? It boggled Pinkoo's mind just to think of it.

'How can they do this to the contestants? I mean, we're nine- to twelve-year-old home bakers, not Jurassic pastry chefs working in five-star hotels,' he cribbed. 'Just my luck—' he broke off to see Manu smiling broadly. 'My life's over and you're smiling?'

PHATT! Manu slapped his back. 'You, my friend, are the luckiest boy in the country.'

Pinkoo was CONFUZZLED. What on earth was he talking about?

'Thank your lucky stars that the sections were shuffled and Nimrat's in your class and you've the chance to be—as the girls say—besties.'

Pinkoo blinked. Manu wasn't making any sense. 'Why on earth would I want to do that?'

'Because she's the owner of Coffee Oye. Because they have the best desserts in town.' Manu paused dramatically. 'Who do you think makes them?'

'Oh my god!' Pinkoo exclaimed. 'Pastry chefs! Nimrat's pastry chefs! If I could train with them ...' he trailed off doubtfully. 'But why would they help me?'

'If you were her bestie, they would.'

'But she's a pestie.'

'Focus, Pinkoo, focus,' Manu coaxed, sounding suspiciously like Coach Aloo. 'Are you going to let a small enmity come in between you and your biggest dream? Or are you going to do whatever it takes to win The Great Junior Bake-a-Thon?'

Pinkoo shook his head. 'No way.'

'Well, do you have a better plan?' Manu challenged.

P O P !

Flashed something in Pinkoo's head. 'Actually, I do!'

CHAPTER 10

It was Monday afternoon and Pinkoo was about to put his better plan into motion. He made his way to the school canteen, Manu and Tutu in tow.

'Out of my way, Ninja Katori, Pinky and his Mini-Me,' Daljit snarled, rudely pushing them out of the way.

Pinkoo made a face. There was no getting away from the villains of the world. But he decided to focus on his plan. He stepped into the canteen and looked around. There she was, sitting alone, eyeing her sandwich critically.

Team Pinkoo marched up to Nimrat's table.

Pinkoo cleared his throat. 'Are these chairs taken?'

Nimrat looked up. 'Why?'

'We wanted to sit on them.'

'Why?'

'Because we don't want to stand and eat.'

She blinked. 'You want to eat here?'

No, on Mars. Pinkoo said aloud, 'Yes, here.'

'Why?'

'I wanted to discuss something with you.'

She put her sandwich down. 'Shoot.'

'That's what I don't want to do, shoot,' Pinkoo muttered.

Nimrat frowned. 'Sorry?'

'Nothing,' Pinkoo said quickly. 'Okay, so, you know all about the barter system, right? Stone Age? History?'

'What about it?'

'I want to trade something with you.'

At last, Nimrat was curious.

'How about I let you do our History project all by yourself? In exchange for something.'

'I was going to do the project all by myself anyway,' Nimrat said evenly.

Pinkoo gnashed his teeth. It was going

to be more difficult than he'd imagined. 'Okay, fine, you can have some something else. Well?'

'I can't think of anything right now. What is it that you want?'

'Your pastry chef.'

'Why?'

'Because googling or YouTubing recipes just won't do.'

'Why?'

'Because everyone else will be doing that. Me, I want professional help.'

'Why?'

'Because I want to perfect my baking skills.'

'Why?'

'Because I want to ace the auditions for The Great Junior Bake-a-Thon.'

'Why?'

'BECAUSE I WANT TO BECOME A PASTRY CHEF!' An irritated Pinkoo yelled.

HUSH! The canteen which was noisier than a fish market fell silent as a library.

'HYUK! HYUK!' Daljit guffawed loudly. 'Did you hear that? He wants to become a pastry chef. He's such a girl!' His henchmen sniggered.

'Hey!' Nimrat shot back, her eyes flashing fire. 'Ever heard of Anthony Bourdain, Jamie Oliver, Gordon Ramsay?'

'They are world famous chefs and they are not girls,' Pinkoo put in.

'Whatever you say, Pinky,' Venom jeered. Titters went up from his table.

Nimrat threw them a dirty look. 'Get up,' she told Pinkoo.

It was his turn to ask, 'Why?'

'Because you need to learn baking from a professional. And those idiots need to learn a lesson.'

S Q U E E E E !

A DELEXCITED Pinkoo nearly started doing cartwheels in the canteen.

Pinkoo and Nimrat made a beeline for the classroom, Manu and Tutu in tow.

‘As you know, I’m the CFO of Coffee Oye.’

Pinkoo scratched his patka. ‘CFO?’

‘Chief Food Officer,’ she explained. ‘Everything goes on the menu only after I approve it.’

The boys looked impressed.

‘We don’t serve too many desserts. But the desserts that we do serve are—’

‘Ace!’ exclaimed Pinkoo.

‘Out of this world,’ agreed Tutu.

‘Mind-blowing,’ whooped Manu.

For the first time ever, Nimrat smiled. ‘We outsource them—’

‘Outsource?’ asked Tutu.

'It means, getting your work done by another person,' she explained.

'Like you outsource your homework to me,' Pinkoo explained with the help of an example.

'Right. So, Mrs Bhalla and Mrs Chaddha supply them,' Nimrat continued.

Pinkoo leapt at the names as though they were bones and he an excited pup. 'Let's tell them ... err, request them.'

'Mrs Chaddha is in the US. She's back only next month.'

'Okay, Mrs Bhalla it is, then.' Pinkoo rubbed his hands in glee.

'Before that,' Nimrat said, holding up a hand. 'Can you bake? At all?'

Pinkoo was super annoyed. It was like asking Virat Kohli if he could bat.

'That's all he can do ...' Tutu began.

'Awful student, average sportsman, awesome chef,' Manu finished.

Pinkoo preened as though he'd received the Nobel Prize in baking.

Nimrat shot him a challenging look. 'Really? Let's see how good you are. Tomorrow. After school.'

'Uh oh!' Pinkoo coloured. He had shooting coaching tomorrow afternoon. Nimrat arched an eyebrow. 'Why? You've got something better to do?'

'Not at all,' Pinkoo said. 'Tomorrow. After school. My place.'

CHAPTER 11

The next afternoon, they were all gathered in Pinkoo's kitchen to catch the action live. They watched as the Super Chef:

Sifted flour, cocoa, baking powder and salt into a bowl and set the mixture aside.

Whipped dollops of butter and spoonfuls of sugar in another bowl.

Whisked eggs into the buttercream.

Blended in coffee powder and vanilla essence.

Poured the molten chocolate in lazy swirls.

Added the flour mixture to the chocolate batter, slowly and gradually.

Stirred in the milk.

Tossed in finely chopped candied almonds and chocolate chips.

Pressed down on the dough with his palm.

Wrapped the flattened dough in plastic and transferred it to the fridge.

The others watched the demo spellbound.

'It'll take forty-five minutes to set,' Pinkoo's voice broke the spell. 'Let's wait outside.'

They trooped out of the kitchen, only to BUMP into someone.

'Beeji!' Tutu exclaimed. 'What are you doing here? I mean, why aren't you at the club?'

'Came home early. Am going for a kirtan,' she replied. 'But what are you all doing here?'

Everyone gulped.

'Beeji, meet Nimrat,' said Pinkoo, recovering fast and first. 'We're working on, erm, a project together.'

'Two projects,' Tutu grinned, piping down as Pinkoo flashed him a warning look.

'Hello, Beeji, I'm Nimrat Bindra.'

'Bindra?' Granny hmmed. 'Simran Bindra's grand-daughter? I play cards with her in the club.'

A sad look crossed Nimrat's face.

'Sorry, puttar, didn't mean to hurt your feelings,' Beeji said instantly.

'Your granny's gone to God?' Tutu asked, eyes as big as Frisbees.

'Tutu!' Beeji admonished him. 'Where are your manners?'

'She's very much alive,' Nimrat said in a small voice. 'But she has stopped talking to us. We-we don't live together anymore.'

Tutu couldn't imagine such a thing. 'But why?'

'Last year, we moved out of our ancestral house,' said Nimrat. 'And my granny was ... is ... really upset about it.'

Grown-ups, bah, they were weird, Pinkoo wanted to say. But he kept his thoughts to himself. As Beeji reached out and pulled Nimrat into a hug, she caught sight of Gurdasji in the kitchen. He was switching on the oven to pre-heat it.

'You're in luck, kids,' she said when they stepped apart. 'Looks like Gurdasji is about to bake his famous goodies.'

The kids exchanged knowing looks.

'Mocha almond cookies, Beeji,' Tutu blabbed, earning a dirty look from Pinkoo.

'They go very well with milk,' she said,

shuffling into the kitchen. 'Will send them to your room. Now, go play.'

'Thanks, Beeji, you're the best,' Pinkoo called out as they made their way to his room.

'You know what, I've decided what I want in exchange,' said Nimrat, leaning against the study table.

Pinkoo went rigid with shock. His autograph book! Of course! Bad, bad, bad idea, leaving it out there, on the table, in the open ...

'I'm not going to give you my autogr—'

'Your beeji,' Nimrat sighed.

Oh, thank god! A super relieved Pinkoo nearly collapsed like a biscuit dunked in hot milk. He adjusted his expression with great difficulty. He didn't want to give her the impression that he didn't care about his granny. He loved her, of course. It's just that autographs were terribly hard to collect.

The next forty minutes passed noisily but peacefully.

'The dough should be ready now,' Pinkoo said, glancing at the clock. 'Will go bake the cookies. See you all in the kitchen in twenty minutes.'

*

Sharp twenty minutes later, Pinkoo offered a freshly baked mocha almond cookie to Nimrat.

She closed her eyes, took a tentative bite and PHATTT! She immediately jetted off to Planet Yum.

The cookie, it was softer than a kitten's fur. (Not that she'd tasted it). Crunchier than a golden toast. Crumblier than a sand castle. Meltier than dewdrops in the morning. Meltier than ice cream on a sultry afternoon. Meltier than ...

'Well,' Pinkoo asked after Nimrat went thought the whole cookie without so much as a PEEP. 'What do you think?'

Her eyes flew open. 'I think we should pay Mrs Bhalla a visit.'

YASSS! Pinkoo started resembling a giraffe doing Gangnam style, err, he started dancing.

Nimat nodded. 'Tomorrow, after school, you and I ...'

Tutu cleared his throat.

'And Tutu,' Pinkoo put in.

Manu coughed.

'And Manu,' Pinkoo added.

Nimrat gave them a thumbs up. 'We'll all pay Mrs Bhalla a visit.'

'I think we should call ourselves something,' Manu suggested. 'How about Fantastic Four? Pinkoo can be Mister Fantastic, Nimrat can be Invisible Girl, I can be Human Torch and Tutu can be The Thing.'

'Or we could come up with better names,' Pinkoo said crossly (as we generally do when someone comes up with a brilliant idea that should have come from us). 'How about Macaroon for Manu, Nutella for Nimrat, Pastry for Pinkoo—'

'—And Tooty Fruity for me,' Tutu yelled.

CHAPTER 12

'You want me to do what?' Mrs Bhalla exclaimed, popping up from the sofa like popcorn.

'I want you to teach me how to bake.'

She crossed her arms over her chest. 'Who has sent you? It's that Menaka Chaddha, isn't it? She thinks she's too smart—'

Pinkoo was CONFUZZLED. 'Who? I don't know any—'

'Aunty,' Nimrat interrupted calmly, 'Bhalla Aunty, may I?'

Mrs Bhalla nodded, looking highly hyper.

'He's Pinkoo, my fr-, err, my desk partner—'

'And project partner,' Pinkoo added as though it was a great qualification.

'He's participating in a contest and he'd like some baking tips. He was looking for a professional pastry chef for help. And I thought who better than you?'

Mrs Bhalla seemed to mellow down at that.

Nimrat flashed her most winning smile. 'You're the best there is. All of Patiala loves your ...'

'Lemon tarts,' Pinkoo volunteered.

'And chocolate mousse,' Manu chimed in.

'And mango soufflé,' Tutu supplied. 'I didn't brush my teeth for two whole days after eating it.'

All eyes swung to him.

'Coming back to my problem,' Pinkoo spoke up. "All I need is some lessons on baking professionally.'

The hostility came flooding back into Mrs Bhalla's eyes. She said, 'So that you can leak my secrets to Menaka Chaddha, my arch rival? So she can supply to Coffee Oye? So she can act like she's the number one baker in town?'

'No, never, Aunty,' Pinkoo protested. 'I have an arch rival, too. I know how it would feel if he stole my autograph book.'

Mrs Bhalla was bewildered. 'What autograph book?'

'My favourite book, it has autographs of all celebrities—Abhinav Bindra, Milkha Singh, Chef Vikas Khanna ...'

'Arre, what are you talking about?'

'Never mind,' Nimrat cut in smoothly. 'Aunty, we're asking you for a teeny favour. Please, please, please help Pinkoo.'

'I'm sorry, Nimi, but I just can't.'

*

'I'm sorry I couldn't help you,' Nimrat said to Pinkoo.

It had been a week since the disastrous visit to Mrs Bhalla.

They were at her house, working on the History project together.

'It's okay,' Pinkoo said glumly. 'I'm confident about the first round, don't mind crashing out after that—'

'Why do you think you'll crash out?' Nimrat broke in.

'Because the second round is all about testing our technical skills. And I don't have any.'

'Oh, I see. I wish I could help,' Nimrat said earnestly.

'Why?' Pinkoo was genuinely curious. After all, she was the same girl who'd made his life difficult, for jumbling up a phrase.

Nimrat shrugged. 'I don't know. Maybe because I like your granny. She's so sweet.'

'Please!' Pinkoo said scornfully. 'She loves bossing over people and expects everyone to obey her commands.'

'Sweet and stern,' Nimrat giggled. 'She sounds like Chef Khanna. Papa's meeting him tomorr—'

GASP! Nimrat stopped talking as an idea hit her. It was brilliant! Why didn't I think of it before, she thought, slapping her forehead.

She turned to Pinkoo, her eyes shining with excitement. 'What are you doing after school tomorrow?'

Pinkoo pouted. 'Shooting practice, what else.'

'Not anymore,' she grinned. 'You're meeting a brilliant pastry chef at Coffee Oye. He used to work with us once upon a time. I'm sure he'll agree to train you.'

Pinkoo looked at her uncertainly. 'If he's so good, why doesn't he work for you anymore?'

'He's retired. He met with a really bad accident a few years ago. He was supposed to move to Canada, but ...' Nimrat sighed. 'Okay, whatever you do, please don't stare at his left hand.'

'Done!' Pinkoo said.

*

It was easier said than done.

Pinkoo found it impossible not to stare at Chef Khanna's left hand. Because he didn't have one. There was just a smooth, dark stump in its place.

'... Ten days away ... please help ... can train him at my place,' Nimrat was telling the retired chef. But Pinkoo didn't hear a single word. He watched in fascination as Chef Khanna went about pouring his tea, stirring in milk and sugar, dunking a cookie. Coolly, calmly.

'Staring at it won't make it grow back, you know,' the chef said dryly.

Pinkoo's eyes flew up. 'I-I'm so sorry, I didn't mean t-to-to—' he stammered, an apologetic expression on his face.

'That's my name, Tutu,' his cousin spoke up.

'Nice to meet you,' Chef Khanna said, before turning his attention back to Nimrat.

'It's a personal request, Chef. Please help us out.'

He raised an eyebrow. 'Us?'

'There's this bunch of stupid guys at school. They think baking is girlie.'

'Hmm,' the retired chef stroked his beard thoughtfully. 'We can't have them thinking that now, can we?'

'So, does that mean—' Pinkoo asked hopefully.

'You've thought of the dessert for Round One, I hear,' replied Chef Khanna.

Pinkoo nodded eagerly.

'Show me.'

CHAPTER 13

The next day, Pinkoo did exactly that.

'All the best,' Bani Aunty, Nimrat's mummyji, said. She hurried away, leaving the Baking Coach and the Fantastic Four alone in the kitchen.

She's so nice, Pinkoo thought, *just like Nimrat*. He chuckled to himself. Nimrat?

Nice? If anyone had said that last month, he'd have gone LOL LOL LOL. *But she was nice. And kind. And helpful,* he thought, as he organized the ingredients and the utensils and the equipment.

'Okay, here's how to make a banana date cake glazed with walnut and honey,' he began, sounding like those famous chefs on TV. 'Mix flour, sugar, butter, eggs, cinnamon and honey.' Pinkoo gave the hand blender a WHIRRR!

'Stop when the batter is light and fluffy.' He set the bowl aside.

'Mash ripe bananas, de-seed dates, chop walnuts ...' he mashed, de-seeded, chopped. '... and slowly add them to the batter.' He stirred them in.

Then, he scooped the batter out. 'Place it in the baking tin and bake for forty-five minutes.'

TINGGGG!

Right on the dot, Pinkoo brought out the cake. He inspected it briefly, before ladling the walnut-honey glaze all over the top. In giddying swirls.

Then, he submitted the answer sheet, err, the cake to the teacher, erm, Chef Khanna.

Four stomachs knotted in worry.

The chef reached for a skewer and pushed it in. It came out clean.

'Yessss!' Manu exulted.

'Yay!' Tutu squealed.

'Thank god,' Nimrat exhaled.

Too early to celebrate, Pinkoo thought worriedly.

Chef Khanna sliced the cake and

popped a piece into his mouth. 'Let's move to Round Two,' he declared.

P H E W W W W W !

Pinkoo finally let out the breath he'd been holding.

*

'What are the skills a pastry chef must possess?' asked Chef Khanna after five days of training.

'PACP,' Pinkoo, who stayed mum whenever the teachers asked questions in class, piped up.

'And it stands for?' the chef prompted, tucking a bowl in the crook of his left elbow and whipping the batter with his right hand.

'P for Planning. A pastry chef should organize all the ingredients in advance. A for Attention to detail. A pastry chef must know the precise measurements. C for Creativity. A pastry chef should experiment and come up with new ideas. P for Patience. A pastry chef must never rush through the steps.' Pinkoo, who always forgot meanings in English, remembered everything.

Chef Khanna transferred the batter to a baking sheet and set the timer on the oven. 'Right. Because baking is a ...'

'Science,' Pinkoo, who scored poorly in Science, replied.

'Correct. In Round Two, the judges will see if ...'

'We've got what it takes to be a real pastry chef,' Pinkoo, who always left the History paper unfinished, finished.

The teacher asked more questions, the student got all of them right.

Why can't school be this much fun, Pinkoo wondered for the hundredth time.

Chef Khanna donned his oven mittens and brought out the baking sheet.

TOINNNGGG! Something suddenly popped into Pinkoo's head. He tossed a question at his baking coach. 'Do you think I've got what it takes?'

The teacher offered the student a bite. 'Why else would we be here,' he replied.

Pinkoo sparkled like a GARGANTUOUS chandelier. The chef's words tasted sweeter than the chocolate fudge he'd just made.

'Thanks, Chef, you're the best!' He really was. Pinkoo was always WOWMAZED at how coolly and normally Chef Khanna went about things. In fact, if someone didn't look too closely, they wouldn't even realize he had only one hand.

'You're awesome into two,' Tutu chirped. 'Because you do everything with one hand.'

Everyone gasped.

Chef Khanna smiled. 'You don't need two strong hands to do anything, just a ...' He tapped his right temple.

'Forehead?' Tutu ventured.

'Strong will. There's nothing you can't do if you put your mind to it.'

*

Later that evening, Pinkoo was sitting in his living room, watching TV with Papaji (and Tutu).

'Puttar,' called out Beeji from her room.

Papaji excused himself and ambled away.

TRINNGGG!

Rang the landline.

Pinkoo's eyes fell on the caller ID and nearly fell out of the socket. It was Coach Aloo! He was calling Papaji! No doubt, to ask why Pinkoo had bunked shooting classes all week!

Pinkoo snatched up the phone. 'Hello? Coach Aloo ... er ... walia?

'Hello? Hello? Is that Pinkoo? I was calling your Papaji to check ... are you okay ... where have been?'

'I-uh, s-s-sorry, Coach ... I was ... down with cold, cough, fever.'

'But you sound fine.'

'But I feel terrible,' Pinkoo replied, making his voice croaky, squeaky, coughy. 'Should feel better in a week.'

'How do you know that?' Coach Aloo retorted. 'You could be better sooner.'

Pinkoo's heart was pounding like a conga. Why couldn't Coach just hang up? 'Doctor's asked me to rest for a week.'

'Oh, I see,' Coach said reluctantly. 'See you soon. Bye.'

WHOOSH! A relieved Pinkoo collapsed like a tent after a storm.

CHAPTER 14

One and a half weeks later, they were at Coffee Oye, busy wolfing down chicken wraps.

Pinkoo felt like Cinderella, erm, Cinderfella. Oh, not because he was wearing a princely outfit or a pair of glass sneakers or gallivanting around in a horse-drawn carriage. Nopesy-daisies. It was just that his fairy godfather had waved his magic spatula and lo! Pinkoo Pumpkin had turned into Pinkoo Pastry Chef.

Before meeting Chef Khanna, he was jittery, stressy, nervy. After meeting Chef Khanna, he was the opposite of jittery, stressy, nervy! He was not going to flunk the biggest exam of his life. He was not going to crash out after Round One. Or Round Two. Or Round Three.

'There's every chance you'll go all the way to London,' Nimrat said the exact same thing that was running through Pinkoo's mind. 'Too bad, your Baking Coach won't be around to see you win the regionals—'

Pinkoo gasped in horror.

A guilty expression came over Nimrat's face. 'Chef Khanna didn't tell you?'

'Tell you what?' asked a familiar voice.

The Fantastic Four looked up to see Chef Khanna smiling down at them.

'You're not coming to Chandigarh?' Pinkoo wailed.

Nimrat put on her 'oopsie' face. The retired chef waved it away.

'I'd have loved to, Pinkoo,' he said earnestly, pulling up a chair and flopping down on it. 'But, I've got to be in Delhi on the same day.'

'But why?'

Chef Khanna drew a deep breath. 'Long story.'

'We're not going anywhere,' said Manu.

'We haven't finished our chicken wraps,' explained Tutu.

'Okay then.' Chef Khanna smiled. 'So, Nimrat's told you about my accident, right. Just before it happened, I was all set to move to—'

'Canada,' Pinkoo cut in. 'She told us.'

'Hmm. But the restaurant withdrew the job offer ... it was a tough time. I decided I didn't want to be a pastry chef anymore. I retired ... started working from home ... I buy and sell shares for people—you know what they are, right? No? Never mind, not important to the story. What is important to the story is that after meeting Pinkoo, after training him, I realized what I was missing out on. I realized I love baking.' He sighed. 'I want to go back to it.'

The Fantastic Four were so shocked, they stopped breathing, erm, eating.

'You've got a job interview in Delhi?' Nimrat squawked.

Chef Khanna nodded.

'Oh my god!' she squealed. 'I thought you were visiting family.'

The next few minutes passed in a chorus of 'All the best!' (Nimrat), 'You'll rock' (Manu), and 'Will we get free dessert in your hotel, Chef?' (Tutu).

Pinkoo stayed mum. Oh, not because he

wasn't happy for his Baking Coach. Because he had a better FANTABULOUS idea! All he had to do was make a call. Easy peasy mac 'n' cheesy.

'Pinkoo, I know you're disappointed,' began Chef Khanna. 'Trust me, I'll be there with you in spirit. I'll be thinking about you. I'll be rooting and praying for you.'

'Thanks, Chef, I know,' Pinkoo said, a silly, billy, smiley pasted over his face.

The chef brought out a package from his bag. 'Here's a little something for you. A thank-you present.'

'For me? I should be buying you one, Chef,' Pinkoo protested, 'you've helped me so much. I haven't done anything—'

'You have, more than you can imagine,' the teacher insisted.

'Aw! Thanks, Chef,' the student accepted.

*

The night before The Great Junior Bake-a-Thon, Pinkoo was busy clearing up after a practise session.

'Is that what you're making for Round Three?' Gurdasji asked, as Pinkoo shut the oven door and set the timer.

'It's too good, no, it's three good ... oh,

you're winning the competition!'

Pinkoo beamed at him. It was rather SCRUMPLICIOUS. He had chosen a killer combo.

'Treat, treat, treat,' Tutu sang out. Pinkoo's lips curled mischievously. 'Here's your treat.' Quick as a flash, he swiped his hand over the messy kitchen counter and leaned over to smear flour across Tutu's cheek.

'EEEEEEEEE!' Tutu yelped, dipping his hands into the large bowl of flour and spraying Pinkoo's face with it.

That's it. A full-on flour fight broke out in the kitchen.

'Why, you—' Pinkoo gasped, chasing him around the kitchen island.

'AAAAAA! Stop!' Tutu shrieked as Pinkoo dunked the entire contents of the bowl on his head. 'Is this how a world famous pastry chef behaves?'

'A what?' came a shocked voice.

The Flour War came to a grinding halt.

Pinkoo froze. It was Papaji!

His mind went blank. Then, a flood of questions came gushing in:

What's Papaji doing at home?

At this time of the day?

How am I going to face him?

He's going to kill me, isn't he?

'Pinkoo,' Papaji's arrow-sharp voice pierced into his thoughts. 'What's going on?'

CHAPTER 15

Tutu vomited the whole story to Papaji. Pinkoo wanted to vomit for real. For once, he couldn't blame his cousin. The look on Papaji's face! He'd seen gentler expressions on Dementors.

The entire Shergill clan was gathered in the living room. Their expressions!

Pinkoo had seen Mummyji look less pained at his PTA meetings. And Beeji, she looked as though she'd lost a card tournament. Even Chachiji was looking up from her cell phone. A rare, rare occurrence indeed.

'Pinkoo,' Papaji spoke at last. 'I thought you were an honest, hard working, obedient boy. But you've been lying to us—'

'I didn't lie,' Pinkoo protested.

'You kept such a big thing from us, that's lying, too ... all this while, I-we thought you were going for shooting practice—'

Pinkoo was unable to contain himself any longer. 'But I hate shooting! I'm sorry, but I hate it!'

TOINGGG!

All mouths hung open.

'Why didn't you say anything all this time?' Papaji asked in a hushed whisper.

'Because I didn't want to hurt your feelings,' said Pinkoo.

'Because he was scared to tell you,' said Tutu.

'I don't want be a world-class shooter, Papaji.' Tears started running down Pinkoo's face. 'I want to be a world famous pastry chef. I don't want to win an Olympic medal. I want to win The Great Junior Bake-a-Thon. Because I love baking!'

'Baking.' Papaji made the word sound like a cockroach. 'I wish I could tell you how

disappointed I am. You've set a bad example for your younger brother and sister, you've let the whole family down—'

'I think that's too harsh,' broke in Beeji, to everyone's surprise. 'Yes, he shouldn't have gone behind our backs, but it's our fault. We shouldn't have pushed him into shooting.'

Papaji was appalled. 'Beeji! You know how much it meant to Pitaji. It was his dream—'

'*His* dream,' she said. 'Not Pinkoo's. We should encourage him to follow his own dream. Is being an average shooter better than being the world's greatest pastry chef?'

'But—'

'I agree with Beeji,' Mummyji said in a firmer voice.

Papaji who was already super shocked, now looked duper shocked.

'Do as you please,' he hissed, storming out of the room.

Pinkoo ran to his granny and threw his arms around her waist. 'What do I do, Beeji?'

'Do your best, puttar,' she murmured, stroking his head. 'Tomorrow, at the competition.'

Then, it was Mummyji's turn to hug him. 'What's for dessert tonight, hmm?' she asked, wiping away his tears.

The dessert! It was almost time! He scurried back to the kitchen.

His mind was like a gaming arcade on a weekend. Packed. Worries were running around in it like boisterous kids. Thoughts were screaming loudly like annoyed parents.

TINGGGG! Went the timer.

Pinkoo opened the oven door, reached inside for the baking tray and—'AAAAAAAAAAAAAA!' he let out a bloodcurdling scream.

Distracted, exhausted, lost in thought, he'd made a rookie mistake. He'd forgotten to pull on the oven mittens!

*

It was a bright and sunny day. Quite naturally, Pinkoo's mood was gloomy and cloudy. Everything had gone horridly horribly, horrifyingly wrong. He was worried that the judges wouldn't give him a chance. That he would be turned away. That his dream would never ever come true.

He'd arrived at Children's Park—the venue of The Great Junior Bake-a-Thon—an hour early. Chachaji had driven the Fantastic Four to Chandigarh (Beeji, Mummyji, Chachiji and Tikki were going to come with Raghav bhaiya. Papaji, of course, wasn't going to come). He'd explained his burnt hands to the organisers. Now it was all up to the judges.

Pinkoo paced outside a huge tent that had been specially constructed for the competition. There was a small stage with baking stations on one end, and chairs for the audience on the other.

A sudden movement caught his eye. He gasped! And took off in the direction of the park's entrance. Manu, Nimrat and Tutu dashed after him.

'Hey, where are you going?' called out Chachaji.

'Chef!' They cried.

Chef Khanna waved, striding up to them. 'I had to be here to cheer my favourite student on,' he smiled.

Pinkoo glowed with pride.

'Oh my god, what happened,' the chef exclaimed, looking at Pinkoo's bandaged hands.

'Long story ...' said Pinkoo.

'Oh no!' Chef Khanna said after Tutu finished narrating the short-cut version. 'That's really unfortunate. Promise me, you'll be more careful in the future. Promise you'll always remember the NONO—No Oven mitts, No Oven—rule.'

Pinkoo nodded glumly.

'Don't lose heart, you still have a chance. We're all here to support you, we'll request the judges—oh, I'm so glad I didn't go to Delhi—'

'You don't have to go to Delhi,' Pinkoo suddenly burst out. 'You can go to Canada!'

CHAPTER 16

Chef Khanna was **CONFUZZLED**. 'Sorry?'

'My Mamiji's family runs a chain of pati-patis—' He trailed away. *Oh, what was that fancy word for pastry shops?*

'Pâtisserie,' supplied Nimrat.

'Yes, that! I've spoken to Mamaji, he's agreed to sponsor you.'

A look of sheer surprise came over Chef Khanna's face. 'Oh, Pinkoo. That's so kind of you. I don't know what to say.'

'Say yes!' chorused the four.

'We'll talk about this after your event.' Chef Khanna smiled and pointed at Pinkoo's clothes. 'I see you liked my gift,' he said.

His student was dressed in white—jacket, pants, hat—the traditional chef's uniform. 'Love it. Thanks again, Chef.'

Nimrat, who was staring the park's entrance, gasped. 'What's Beeji doing here?'

My family's here, yay-ed Pinkoo silently. 'She wanted to watch me in action,' he explained.

'Not your beeji, my beeji!'

Pinkoo turned to see Beeji, Mummyji, Chachiji, Tikki and a stranger—a big bear of a granny—hurrying up to them.

Nimrat dashed up to the big bear granny, halting abruptly, an unsure expression on her face. The big bear granny then rushed forward to give her a big bear hug.

The crying, smiling, kissing and hugging would have continued, but CRACKLE! went the microphone.

'Hello and welcome to the regional auditions of The Great Junior Bake-a-Thon: Indian Edition!' came the compere's voice.

'Ready?' Chef Khanna asked Pinkoo.

'Born ready,' he replied.

Off they went to the tent!

'... I'm sure most of you are familiar with the format of the contest,' the compere was saying. 'As you know, we have three rounds. Our judges will take you through them. Please put your hands together for Chef William ...'

A tall, thin man sporting a ponytail ambled on to the stage. Pinkoo recognized him right away. He was one of the judges

on TGJBT! He'd flown in all

the way from London! Oh, it was finally starting to feel real!

'... and Chef Malhotra.'

CLAPS! CHEERS!

WHISTLES!

The compere handed over the mike and the stage to them.

'Thank you for being such a wonderful audience,' Chef William beamed. 'I am delighted to see such a fabulous turnout. May we have all the contestants on stage, please?'

A bunch of eager bakers trotted onto the stage.

'Let's hear it for our thirty-five contestants—'

Chef Malhotra had been checking the list of participants, and whispered something in his ear.

'Sorry, thirty-six,' Chef William corrected himself. 'We have a very unusual situation here. One of our contestants'—he bent down to peer at the sheet—'Mr Pinkoo Shergill ended up burning his hands in a baking accident last night ...'

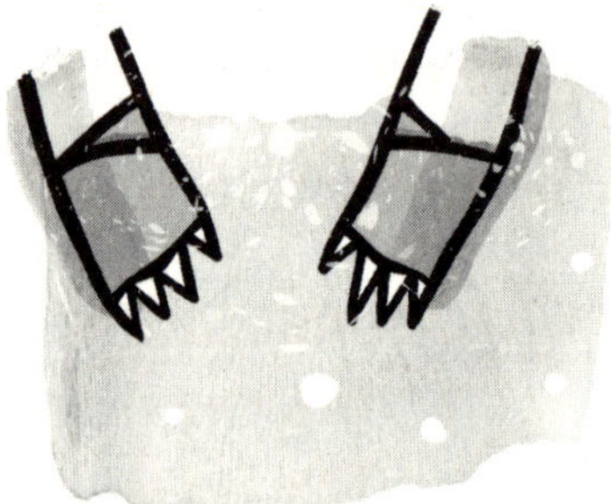

GASPS! MURMURS!
WHISPERS!

'... but he'd still like to participate. Oh, I don't know about that ...'

'Please, judges,' Pinkoo called out from the audience, bringing his bandaged hands together.

The judges exchanged a look. 'But how will you manage—'

'You don't need two strong hands to do anything,' Pinkoo replied in a brave voice, glancing at Chef Khanna. 'Just a strong will.'

CLAPS! CHEERS!
WHISTLES!

'Give us a few minutes,' said Chef Malhotra. 'We'll be back with a decision.'

The judges were about to put their heads together, when Tutu put his hand up. 'Idea! I can be Pinkoo paaji's runner!'

The judges gaped at him. 'The what?'

'In cricket, if a batsman is injured, he gets a runner,' Tutu began. 'He still hits the shots, but the runner runs between the wickets for him. I'm Pinkoo paaji's susu chef, I know what he's making for all the rounds.'

'Pinkoo's the best pastry chef in all of Patiala,' called out Manu.

'He's worked really hard for this,' chimed in Nimrat.

'He's gone against his father's wishes to be here,' added Mummyji.

'Please give him a chance,' echoed Beeji.

'Please, please, please,' said Chachaji and Chachiji.

The judges went into a huddle.

'Do the other participants have any objection to this?' Chef Malhotra asked at last.

Pinkoo's eyes swept over the crowd, his stomach in knots.

Not a single hand went flying up! Not a single voice cried out, 'Not fair! Chuck him out!' Not a single objection!

'Okay, Mr Shergill,' piped up Chef William, 'you're on.'

ZINGGG! A HAPPYXCITED Pinkoo catapulted himself onto the stage.

'All right, let's begin,' said Chef Malhotra. 'Round One: Chef's Special. Will the first six contestants please step up to the baking stations? It's time to whip up your favourite dessert ...'

*

Before long, it was Pinkoo's turn. He took a deep breath and walked to the baking station, butterflies in stomach, Tutu in tow.

THWACK! The batsman hit the shot and the runner scampered between the wickets.

'... Whip the batter, whip it some more ... now add the flour mixture, slowly and gradually ... yes, good, like that ...' For the next hour, Pinkoo shouted the instructions and Tutu followed them to the T.

RINNGGG!

Went the bell.

'One second, one second,' Pinkoo beseeched like a student in an exam hall, who wants to revise one last time. Alas! The teachers marched to his desk to collect the answer sheet.

CHAPTER 17

He watched as the judges inspected and tasted and rated the cake.

The next few minutes! As stressful as waiting for the annual exam report card!

Presently, Chef Malhotra cleared his throat. 'Okay, we have the results. We were looking for presentation, creativity, taste. Here are the contestants who got all three right ...'

Pinkoo's stomach lurched.

'Mohita Chawla! Your raspberry pear soufflé was out of this world. Light, fluffy, not too eggy, not too leathery. Just perfect!'

'Aruna Manchanda! I don't have words to describe your dark chocolate mousse topped with whipped cream. It was like tasting a chocolate cloud!'

'Riya Gulati! Your bite-sized cake pops, dipped in melted candy, packed a big bite. Sheer indulgence on a stick.'

'Sanaya Vij! Your fruit cream trifle blew our minds. Sinfully creamy, divinely rich, refreshingly wholesome.'

'Nitika Diwan! Your pink glazed donuts, dusted with sprinkles, were fun and phenomenal!'

'And finally ...'

Pinkoo stopped breathing. It was now or never. Would he, wouldn't he?

'Pinkoo Shergill! Take a bow. Your banana cake with honey and almond glaze was a slice of heaven!'

WHOOSSH! An ecstatic Pinkoo floated away to seventh heaven.

Chef William clapped his hands. 'Great show, everyone! Moving on to Round Two: Chocolate Surprise. We'll give you minimum instructions and a maximum of sixty minutes to make the same dessert. Now listen closely ...'

Pinkoo did.

An hour later, the six contestants (and Tutu) were standing next to their chocolate-filled puff pastries.

The judges went from baking station to baking station. Examining, tasting, discussing, scribbling.

'Okay,' Chef Malhotra said after a while. 'In this round, we were looking for precision and artistic flair. And the three finalists are ... well, any guesses?'

'Pinkoo!' bellowed Manu and Nimrat.

'Will the incredibly talented Mohita Chawla please step forward?'

Mohita's hands flew to her face.

'Let's hear it for Riya Gulati! Her sense of proportion and taste really shine through.'

Riya whooped and punched the air.

'Last but not the least, Pinkoo Shergill! His creations are edible art!'

'YAHOOOO!' Manu hollered, leaping to his feet.

Team Shergill burst into applause. Mummyji burst into tears.

Chef William looked the finalists. 'Let's take a short lunch break. See you in a bit,' he told the hungry audience. 'In the meantime, we'll get to know our three finalists better.'

*

A good one hour later, the super stuffed audience and the super stressed finalists were back in place.

'And we're back for Round Three: Indian Twist. Time to blend East and West and come up with your best. Remember, the winner will go to Mumbai to compete in the Finals. Ready, pastry chefs? Your time starts now.'

The three finalists (and Tutu) went to work on their masterpieces.

P I N G G G G !

'And the time's up! Let's see what we have here,' said Chef William, sauntering up to Mohita.

'Motichoor laddu and white chocolate brownie,' said Mohita.

'Sounds yummy! Riya?'

'Cupcakes with strawberry shrikhand frosting.'

'Delicious, delectable. Pinkoo?

'Gulab jamun cheesecake.'

'The mouth waters. We'll be back with the results soon.'

As the judges went about their work, Pinkoo's eyes went to the audience.

THUDDD! Pinkoo's jaw hit the floor. Was that Papaji in the last row? How long had he been sitting there? He'd been so engrossed in his cheesecake, he hadn't noticed Papaji come in.

'Ladies and gentlemen,' announced Chef Malhotra, 'it's here. The moment you've been waiting for.'

Pinkoo forced himself to concentrate on what the judges were saying.

'And the winner is ...'

Pinkoo held his breath.

'Motichoor laddu and white chocolate brownie!'

The spectators were on their feet, applauding, chanting, cheering. It was just like in Pinkoo's dream. Except, they weren't chanting his name. They were saying, 'Mohita! Mohita! Mohita!'

Was he heartbroken? Nopesy-daisies. His heart was soaring. Papaji wasn't angry with him anymore! He hadn't stayed away! He'd come to cheer for him, on the most important day of his life!

Pinkoo dashed down the steps, ran to the last row and threw his arms around his father.

'I'm so sorry, Papaji. I shouldn't have lied to you.'

'No, I'm sorry, Pinkoo,' Papaji said, squeezing him tight. 'I was wrong. You belong in the kitchen, on stage, on TV. Pinkoo Shergill Pastry Chef, I'm so, so, so proud of you.'

'But I didn't win,' Pinkoo said, as they stepped apart.

'Winning, losing, that's secondary. What matters is that you didn't give up. You came all the way to Chandigarh, you gave it your best shot. You're a true champion.'

Pinkoo was **WOWMAZED** to hear that. 'Thanks a lot, Papaji. I'd never want to disappoint you.'

His father's face lit up. 'Really? Then, how about you bake on weekdays and go for shooting classes on weekends?' He burst out laughing at Pinkoo's horrified expression. 'Just kidding.'

'Too bad, the Shergills won't be bringing home any shooting medals,' Pinkoo joked back.

THAYN! THAYN! Tikki approached them, firing her toy gun at an unsuspecting victim, finding her mark.

'Oh, I think they will,' Papaji murmured, looking at her with new eyes.

By the time Team Shergill joined them, Papaji had already imagined Tikki winning the gold at the World Shooting Championships *and* the Olympics.

reat Junior
Bake-A-Thon

GLOSSARY

Puttar –	Son
Chachiji –	Dad's younger brother's wife
Tayiji –	Dad's older brother's wife
Mamaji –	Mom's brother
Chachaji –	Dad's younger brother
Tayaji –	Dad's older brother
Paaji –	Older brother
Djembe –	African drum
Nagada –	Indian kettle drums
Golmaal –	Mischief
Galti –	Mistake
Patka –	Small turban
Kirtan –	A group of people singing devotional songs
Conga –	Cuban drum
Mamiji –	Mom's brother's wife

ACKNOWLEDGEMENTS

Thank you, thank you, thank you. To all the wonderful ingredients that went into making this book.

To MY FAMILY: Flour.

To MY EDITOR, SUSHMITA: Sugar.

To MY ILLUSTRATOR, SHAMIKA: Baking soda.

To MY PUBLISHER, SHANTANU,
AND TEAM SCHOLASTIC: Butter.

To MY FRIENDS: Vanilla essence.

To MY READERS: The cherry on top.

To HP: Oven mitts.

ABOUT THE AUTHOR

Vibha Batra writes for children, young adults, adults and senior citizens. She can be found in quaint cafes in Chennai, hunched over her laptop, typing away like a woman possessed or on FB: facebook/vibhy.batra or Instagram: @vibhybatra.

ABOUT THE ILLUSTRATOR

Shamika Chaves is a children's book illustrator and graphic designer based in Mumbai, India. She has also worked as a comic artist and enjoys character design and handtype. Her illustrated books have been nominated for the Neev Book Awards in 2018 and 2019. She lives and works in her cosy little home with her husband, Christopher and their seven-year-old tortoise, Sebastian. Visit @shamikasdoodles on Instagram or www.shamikasdoodles.com to learn more about her work.